W9-CYW-948

# Cuban Country Food

### More than rice and beans

© Eddy Fernández Monte, **2015**
© Miriam Rubiel Díaz, **2015**

**Executive editor:** Iris Gorostola
**Edition and correction:** EnaDomech
**Photographs:** Julio A. Alvite Piedra
**Design and Layout:** Dieiker Bernal Fraga
**Prepress and impression:** Selvi Artes Gráficas

Translation Ana V, Portela

**ISBN: 978-84-944860-5-0**
Selvi Ediciones
Director: Miguel Selvi Garayoa
Selvi Artes Gráficas. M. Selvi S.A.
Calle Miguel Selvi Cariñena, 22-24 • 46469 Beniparrell (Valencia) España
www.graficasselvi.com • www.selviediciones.com
info@selviediciones.com

Editorial Artechef
Director: Eddy Fernández Monte
Adddress:: Habana No. 304 e/ O'Reilly y San Juan de Dios. Habana Vieja
www.arteculinario.cu
culinaria@enet.cu

All Rights are reserved. No part of this book can be reproduced, stored or transmitted in any way by any means, be it electronically, mechanically, optically, magnetic recorded or xerographed without authorization of the author and editorial house for the agreed upon time.

# Cuban Country Food

### More than rice and beans

CHEF EDDY FERNÁNDEZ MONTE
LIC. MIRIAM RUBIEL DÍAZ

# Table of contents

## Complementary recipes /76

## Technical vocabulary /78

## Weights, measures and equivalents /79

## Table of equivalents /79

# Prologue
## Basket of Evocations

For reasons undoubtedly justified, the Spanish draftsman of local customs, Víctor Patricio Landaluze (1828-1889) created the guajiros as an image of the Cuban people, later transformed by Ricardo de la Torriente (1867-1934)t into the personage, Liborio,

This unique concept later became the symbol of the campesino of the dispossessed classes and later became popular to evoke the frustrations of the people at the end of the epic independence war, during the United States intervention and the pseudo republic. Today it refers to the community of interests that bind people and State.

And why guajiros? This generalized version of the corrupted phonetic word: warhero. An expression that appears after 1895 in Cuban literature, In the vast literary work of Juan Cristóbal Nápoles Fajardo, "El Cucalambé" (1829-1861), it is the usual form in a fragment of a **Cock Fighting Ring**:

*rich and poor men*
*gather around*
*democratically and argue*
*About spurs and beaks,*
*Between large and small*
*The unhappy craftsman;*
*In a human gathering,*
*There is no person alive*
*Who adores more the cock ring*
*Than the Cuban guajiros.*

It is about those who live tied to their origins, to the place they would prefer to be, of persons with material humility and simple desires, with natural sense and well forged in daily life. Men and women with their own culture; whose *modus vivendi* has secularly represented a challenge to the logic of existence. They live in houses built with what is available: boards, beams, posts, sawhorses and native wooden planks cured on the land, roofed with a complicated mesh of palm leaves, a sort of monument to architecture in tune with nature.

Entering a typical campesino home often reveals a meeting with affectionate memories: furniture of unrecognizable styles or dates of manufacture but seen with the unavoidable "I don't remember where" interior decoration with a familiar fragrance that make us feel a part of it; photos in grey and sepia tones; religious images; social realities and diverse social tastes placed in curious arrangement; curtains instead of doors to the bedrooms that permanently offer confidence and respect for the awaited visitor; kitchen, dining room bathrooms located prudently apart from other parts of the house, with an instinctive demonstration of "everything in its place". All disposed under the condition of the indispensible and no room for the unnecessary.

With similar logic are placed outside the rural home. In front a guiro plant, appreciated for the use of its fruits, the use of its pulp for medicinal purposes and the possibility of making a cup, once dried, for food and beverages. Steaming coffee will never taste the same in a fine English porcelain cup than a rustic *jicarita*.

The Campesino identified the act of planting this tree with the birth of a girl so that when she grows up, the boyfriend, in pre matrimonial courtship has where to tie his horse. Also, "in front ornamental flowers are planted forming natural fences with cardon (thistles), espina de rayo or espanta-ladrones as well as medicinal plants. These are visible to anyone so a person would know where to find them and, with proper permission, obtain the well appreciated cutting.

In all intents to keep the house clean, at the entrance an old machete held in its ends with two small trunks as a subjective symbol indicating the removal of mud accumulated in the soles of the boots. On the side the dogs of the home, with warning barks present their credentials as efficient guardians until the master indicates the treatment to follow with the new arrivals.

The backyard has the customary sour orange tree with an orchid on its trunk. Other fruit trees offer shade, tranquility and rich menus while the natural spaces are set aside for raising pigs and chickens. Shacks for agricultural tools of different use and season, and clotheslines set up on cane stalks – that serve to dry clothes in sunlight, complete the multipurpose area, that can also serve as well as a workshop or relaxation area.

Not only for its dignified figure is the palm tree represented in the national shield. It is a symbol of natural alliance with the countryside for those who live there. As well as the roof for the campesino and food for smaller animals, the fibers of the leaves are used to make the campesino hat and everything that symbolizes Cuba. The machete that was used as a weapon is also a vital tool. In the manner of carrying it distinguishes the warrior and workers of the land.

### Eat "a lo campesino"

The type of gastronomic service known as the Cuban school of hospitality in which *a la Española* – is the placement of trays, serving dishes, vegetables and even cauldrons in the center of the table for guests to serve at will – also called *a la Campesina, a la Criolla or a la Cubana.*

Certainly the manner of making fires in rural Cuba have distinctive qualities. The diet of the campesino has certain common features reminiscent of the African slave population: eating food of high energy value; these include rice and viands as well as salted and dried meat like in *tasajo* and heavily sweetened deserts. They use natural woods and wood carbon to achieve the excellent authenticity of aromas and tastes

The preference for pig meat relies primarily on it being a smaller livestock, less cost of production and ease of raising. Its assimilation to national taste – even in celebration meals – is proof of the insertion of the campesino as an essential component of native gastronomic identity. Even the form of seasoning (marinade using sour oranges, garlic and salt) and roasting in a pit (the pig traversed longitudinally with a pole [either iron or wood] held at the ends by two forks to help turning it over the wood or carbon fires) has a local and regional practice typical of traditional Cuban cooking.

The killing of a pig in the countryside is not a festivity. In its most authentic manner it marks the beginning of a laborious process of conservation and consumption: the animal is cut in pieces to fry in its own fat and later placed in wooden barrels, or metal or plastic tanks where it can be stored in fat without refrigeration. Other meats present in the campesino menu is lamb in the eastern region of the country; goat and guanajo (Cuban name for turkey) and duck. The hutia is also typical of rural gastronomy, however, there is a policy strongly protecting it since it is an endangered species.

Water species are not excluded from typical rural cooking. Aside from the relaxing pleasure of fishing one day and waiting with a fish pole of bamboo at the shore of a river or stream, lagoon or reservoir to catch sweet water tilapia or trout that also are part of the diet in the countryside. The advances of native techno sciences has contributed to diversify work and food habits of the rural population or in different regions of the country with the development of aquiculture, without affecting fishing populations who obtain their food in coastal regions.

With great estimation are the native eggs, recognized by the intense color of the yolks due to the natural food for raising hens. The same occurs with the characteristic firm texture and taste typical of chickens and hens.

Natural also is the seasoning with a predominance of sour oranges, lemon and aromatic herbs: oregano and coriander, as well as an interminable list of vegetable curing remedies for pains and ills, both for people as for animals.

*Verbena cimarrona, bejuco ubí, flor de España, caña santa, orange leaves, garlic, piña de ratón, menta piperita, hierba buena, caisimón, toronjil, apazote, manzanilla and tilo* are also examples of an encyclopedic medical knowledge in the Cuban countryside.

A nation made of sweetness, both for its vegetable species as for its people; fruits are important, eaten both fresh and in delicious homemade desserts. A similar relevance is the use of lemon as an additive, present in the classic Cuban cocktails. In addition is the use of oranges, pineapple, grapefruit and coconut as well as the *aguardiente* (liquors) and rums.

In the battlefields of the 19th century in Cuba there was a beverage favored by the independence fighters considered a beverage that excites: the canchanchara, based on aguardiente, lemon juice and honey. Even with a dash of pepper.

In the Eastern region of Oriente is the *aliñao*. It represents a gastronomic solution to life since preparation begins when pregnancy of the future mother is confirmed; it is stored during gestation, (preferably buried under ground or in a dark place) and is offered to the family members and friends who visit the newborn. Preparation is prolonged by separating a portion to continue marinating until the festivities of the coming out of 15 year old girls and later for the wedding of the daughters.

It is made by crushing several fruits, dried or fresh or previously cooked in syrup of aguardiente. Fruits commonly used are red currants, Chinese prunes (*carambola*), plums, raisins as well as pieces of pineapple, papaya and any other foreign fruit such as tinned figs, apples and pears.

The meal concludes with coffee and tobacco, ingredients so genuine in the daily life of the nation. The coffee is strained piping hot into a cloth sleeve over a wooden stand and drunk in small enamel jugs without nicks due to daily use: and the other, rolled tobacco over the leg of the farmer during the meal, lighted with a hot carbon coal. Later, sit in a stool leaning back against the wall or trunk of a tree and have no doubt confusing the Cuban act with the sensation of touching the sky with the fingers.

*Jorge Méndez Rodríguez-Arencibia*

# Of rices, viands and vegetables...

## RICE
*"Neither gooey or smoked"*

Rice constitutes an important part in the food of the slaves together with bacalao (dried and salted codfish), tasajo (beef jerky) plantains, flour, sweet potato and potatoes. Little by little it found its way to the Cuban table, regardless of their social and economic class, to the point that a meal without rice is unthought-of.

This first item in the gastronomic preferences of the population is eaten as a main dish, if combined with certain proteins, in garnishes (white, moros cristianos) and made in deserts.

## AJIACO (STEWS), BEAN STEWS AND SOUPS
*"From the plate to the mouth the soup cools"*

Ajiaco is a thick stew made with different kinds of meat, pieces of viands that include plantains, yucca, squash and sweet potato. To complete the termination adding lemon juice and green pepper. This is considered a typical dish of Camagüey that initially was accompanied by cassava, an aboriginal dish prepared with yucca.

The potaje (bean stew) as well as soups are made from a base consume. It is prepared with dried vegetables, mostly black beans, kidney beans, white beans, garbanzo, peas, gandul and lentils.

Having meats, bacon, green, fresh and dried vegetables of a high nutritional value contains almost all the elements necessary for a complete balanced diet. Depending on the type of beans certain viands and vegetables can be added: potatoes, squash, malanga, cabbage, turnips, and swiss chard.

A soup is prepared with a type of broth in which vegetables and meats have been cooked. Due to its low caloric density it is considered good to reduce stomach problems and contributes to a healthy diet. Usually it is eaten at the beginning and allows using byproducts of meats, fish, vegetables and pastas; although other foods can be used.

According to their feature and consistency they can be clear (consumes and clear soups) or combined soups (soups, purees, creams and velouté [white sauce]), They can be eaten hot or cold.

Traditionally hen broth is a very useful food for post-partum women. It is made cutting the hen in parts, boning and boiling with garlic and sour oranges. This broth is also used for sick people and convalescents from several illnesses.

# MEATS
*"Meat close to the bone, give me that"*

Livestock is a group of animals (mostly mammals) raised by man to produce meat and its byproducts that are used in human nutrition.

Meats are classified according to color in reds and whites. In the first are pork, beef, lamb and the second are fowl and rabbit.

### Pork
*"Winter would be good if the pig slaughtered is large or small."*

When the mammal is small and has not yet been weaned it receives the name of lechal or lechón. Later it is called hog, pork, pig or *macho* according to different regions of the country. Today it is very favored by Cubans. Its use has a large history and is the most useful meat using all parts of the animal and serves as a main dish in many recipes. It can also be mixed with other products obtaining a variety of sausages and such large imaginative preparations. Some are made by the campesino who raises them. During campesino festivities it is roasted or fried.

### Beef
*"Without broth, the meat is good"*

is the preferred meat of persons becoming one of the main food products of humanity. It has a high content of proteins, fat, usable substances, minerals and vitamins. Although according to recent research its excessive consumption can raise the level of uric acid in blood.

Age groups are divided into 2.5 to 3 months and 1 year old which is calf, 2 to 3 years, young bull, buey (oxen) or cow.

Among the recipes offered in this group are preparations with a variety of cuts such as steak, minced, diced, filets that and cooked over a grille, in stews, roasted and pasties.

Tasajo is a processed meat that is soaked and hydrated. Once processed it is boiled and prepared in different forms.

### Mutton and lamb
*"The bass from the sea and lamb from the earth"*

It received the name of lamb until it reaches the age of one when it is called mutton or sheep. An optimum yield of these animals depends on the high grade of its age, sex, nutrition and fattening. Its quality is known by the width of its kidneys that should be covered by a very compact meat. Freshness is found by the hardness of the thigh and light pink color. Also goat is very much appreciated and reaches the same quality in preparations used for lamb.

Usually the entire sheep is used in different preparations of stews with ribs, breast bone and shank. Select dishes use leg of lamb.

### Rabbit

*"When least expected it runs off"*

Rabbits are raised by the campesino in his yards, in cages he has made himself. For culinary preparations this exquisite animal must be four or five months of age. Its taste depends largely on its food. The cuts are simple: in eighth inch portions, quartered or whole. It is used in stews or roasted and in other very special preparations it is fried. Also important is the liver for exquisite dishes.

### Fowl

*"You eat what the chicken pecks"*

All the time the campesino has raised domestic animals, mostly chicken, turkey (guanajo), guinea hen and duck. He eats the tasty meat and also another product, the egg.

A lunch for Cubans can be fried, scrambles eggs or omelets, Eggs can be boiled or stewed and is a form of enjoying a good breakfast. It is also used for baking and in deserts such as puddings and flans. Nutritionists assume that two large eggs can substitute for 100 grams of meat. At the same time one must not abuse its consumption since it is rich in cholesterol.

The gizzards or sub products: wings, sweetbread, liver, neck, heart and legs are used in broths, soups and other preparations.

In the western part of the country it is common practice to smoke these meats: in the central region it is preferred grilled and roasts and in the easternmost region, in stews.

Of the different species of fowl most important is the chicken that is commonly cooked. Generally is seasoned with salt and white pepper but also with black pepper when prepared with dark sauces. The criollo way of cooking is seasoned with lemon or sour oranges and a dash of garlic. When used for stews or braised. Another complement is to marinate with wine, onion, laurel leaves and oregano, with other possibilities.

## VEGETABLES

*"Salad for the taste buds should always be on the table"*

In the plots the campesino usually has some plants for the preparation of salads that are seasoned with lemon juice, salt and oil to taste. Salads are usually tomato, avocado, lettuce, cucumber, watercress and others.

Corn is part of this wide family; it is grown in our fields and served as a basis for the campesino. Often it is used to feed the animals in their farms.

It is healthy and contributes nutritional proteins, fat, fibers, calories, carbon hydrates and minerals. It is used in many preparations such as stews, fritters, tamales, soups and other forms.

# VIANDS

*"With foreign viands, the meal does not cost"*

These are the crops that contribute to strengthen human nutrition. It is applied to a group of fruits and roots rich in carbohydrates, such as the yucca, squash, plantains, potato, sweet potato and malanga.

Among their characteristics is the large quantity of water that is a minimum density of nutrients as well as a low content of proteins. At the same time they supply energy and are a complement to other foods contributing a balance in the diet. Viands can be prepared alone or combined in many manners: boiled, fritters stews and soups, as well as other dishes.

# FRUITS

*"When hungry in heat:*
*beverage and juice is better"*

In Cuba there is a large variety of fruits used to prepared delicious beverages, milk shakes and the so well known "homemade desserts" that are prepared in syrups such guava shells, grapefruit and oranges, shredded coconut, papaya dessert and others.

Cuban tastes are conditioned for relatively high content of sugar and is not only used in the preparation of deserts but also in foods in which the practice of added a dash of sugar to the stews is common.

Also very common is adding an excess of sugar to juices, beverages, milkshakes and coffee. Also common is the guarapo a juice made by crushing sugar cane and adding ice. It is very nutritive and delicious.

# COFFE IN CAMPESINO COOKING

*"Time erases everything even coffee is erased"*

There is nothing better for a Cuban than a little cup of coffee, at any hour of the day, in breakfast it tastes like glory and after meals it is the satisfaction of eating well.

The coffee is picked in the fields when the bean is ripe; it is peeled and set to dry for several days in the sun and in high places. When dry it is stored in proper jars and squashed according to its consumption. The bean is roasted in a deep caldron with a dash of sugar and stirred constantly.

Afterwards it is ground in a deep wooden bowl of about a meter in height and 45 cm deep and width. A half a meter long mace of hard wood is used to crush the coffee until completely ground. Later it is stored in tight covered jars to conserve the aroma and quality of the grain.

To make it the campesino places the ground coffee in water to heat and strain in teapots after sweetening with honey, dark or white sugar. Today it is very common to use Italian coffeemakers and electric coffee makers.

The regions where it is more common to grow coffee in Cuba are: Taco Taco, Candelaria and San Cristóbal in the province of Pinar del Río; in Villa Clara, Trinidad, Guantánamo and mountain eastern regions such as Yateras, San Luis and the Sierra Maestra.

# Herbs and Seasonings...

## PEPPERS

*"If hot it is because you eat peppers"*

It is an herbaceous plant flowering permanently in natural conditions, but planted annually in most cases due to its susceptibility to frost, and damages in cold weather. Today it is eaten fresh, fried or roasted, in conservation and in powder, crushed or ground.

The most practical classification is based on the fruits as regards position, size and form. The guaguao pepper, capsicum, cachucha (used most in pickles) the chay (preferentially used as a seasoning; it is small – 2 to 3 inches long and conical). It is the most commonly used in our country as a daily seasoning.

It has medicinal properties: applied on the skin to eliminate pain in patients with arthritis, herpes zoster. diabetic neuropathy, mastectomy and headaches. It is a good source of most vitamins B, especially B6. They are rich in potassium, magnesium and iron.

## GARLIC

*"With bread and raw garlic you are assured a tasty treat"*

This plant is well known for its root bulb that we know as head of garlic, it has garlic cloves that contain its nutritional value properties, high in vitamins (B1, B3 and C) as well as proteins glysides, calories, water, Niacin, lipids, iron, potassium, calcium and phosphorous.

There are many ways to peel the cloves. One is to peel the skin by hand; another is to introduce in boiling water for 30 seconds that is easily peeled and another way is using a knife, but we must place the garlic on a board, and crush the clove with the blade that helps in removing the skin.

This species can be used, ground, crushed, cut and whole; in snacks, marinades, soups and stews, salads, in pickles, seasonings, mojos, sauces, and preparations of meats, fowl and fish.

It has magnificent medicinal properties due to its bactericidal substances that combat different infections as a disinfectant, a stimulant and diuretic. It is used to calm some respiratory and rheumatic illnesses. It is important to use raw since in cooking it may weaken some of its properties and nutritional value. There are those who claim it increases longevity if eating one clove a day.

## BIJA

*"As a colorant and medicinal properties it is exceptional"*

Bija also known as Achiote, grows in warm regions of America. It can reach 8 meters in height. It has red flowers at the end of the branch. It blooms in September but the flowers fall soon. The fruit is a capsule with two valves, fleshy, oval, covered in flexible spines and has many seeds adhered to a bright red fine dust. Previously the natives crushed the seeds to obtain a red substance with which they decorated their bodies.

## ONION

*"Fell in the pot for the sweet onion"*

It is used as a seasoning, alone or with other herbs giving the food a specific taste. It is a plant that is never missing in a dish served in a campesino table.

There are many varieties of onions and their bulbs are of different shapes and colors. It is used in salads, broths, rices, stews, different preparations of meats: fish, beef, pork and fowls; for mixed seasonings it is essential also for different kinds of sauces. It is always delicious, either pickled, fried, breaded, boiled, roasted or raw. It is beneficial for health eaten raw since cooking destroys some substances necessary for nutrition.

To store in vinegar, well cleaned and skinned they are introduced into a glass jar and cooked for 2 to 5 minutes in 1 cup of vinegar , to two cups of water, 2 tablespoons of salt and one of sugar. This liquid is introduced in the jar with the onions. The jar is closed and placed in water to cook for 20 minutes.

They must be stored in a dry and well ventilated place avoiding direct sunlight that can rot the preparation.

It is a food with low energy value and very rich in mineral salts. It has vitamins A, B and C.

## CORIANDER
*"Coriander is good… but not too much"*

The coriander plant is of the same family as the carrot, anise, parsley and dill. It is grown mostly for its leaves and aromatic seeds. The leaves are used as a common ingredient in Asian and American cuisine. The seeds provide an oil used in liquors.

## LAUREL
*"Whoever plants a laurel will not sit in its shade"*

Laurel is a small tree. It is frequently used as a seasoning, and is greatly appreciated for its digestive and anti rheumatic properties.

## OREGANO OF THE SOIL
*"Not all the countryside is oregano"*

Origanumvulgare is commonly called oregano. The leaves of this plant are used as a seasoning, either dried or fresh although they have more taste and aroma if dried.

The plant has little glands that contain the aromatic essence of a lemon yellow color.

## TOMATO
*"If we have tomatoes and eggs we will not go hungry"*

The tomato is very easy to grow in Cuba; in different soils and sometimes wild. If the residual elements of the washing are placed in a patio or some area of the house, in a few days the plant grows with very green leaves.

Many dishes are prepared with this plant due to the taste it gives the preparation. It is one of the most popular ingredients because of its versatility and ease of combining with cheeses, eggs, meats and a wide variety of aromatic herbs.

It is rich in vitamin C. It is also a very important source of a red pigment called licopene and has anti oxidant properties and may be anti carcinogenic.

# White Rice

## INGREDIENTS

350 g. of rice
500 ml. of water
45 ml. oil
Salt to taste

## PREPARATION

Eliminate impurities and wash well. Boil the water with salt and oil. Add the rice and mix well. Continue cooking until it begins to dry and continue to cook in the oven until completely soft.

### Note

This can be used as a garnish for other preparations, accompanying other dishes.

# Rice with Squash

## INGREDIENTS

350 g. of rice
160 g. of squash
90 g. criollo sauce
24 ml. of oil
60 ml. dry wine
3 g. of bija
500 ml. of water
Salt to taste

## PREPARATION

Cut the squash in small pieces. Prepare salsa criollo. Heat water to boiling. Add the rice, squash, salsa criolla, salt, bija and oil. Continue cooking until dried. Continue cooking in the oven until the rice is completely soft. Add wine and conclude cooking.

# Rice with Crackling

## INGREDIENTS

350 g. of rice
460 g. crackling
60 g. onion
8 g. garlic
70 g. pepper
70 g. fresh tomato
45 ml. oil
500 ml. White broth
Salt to taste

## PREPARATION

Wash rice. Clean and cut à la jardinière. In the pot where the rice will be cooked, fry the herbs in oil. Add the crackling and rice, stir for 2 to 3 minutes. Add hot broth and salt. When boiling begins, stir thoroughly and cover until cooking is done

# Rice with Pork

## INGREDIENTS

350 g. of rice
580 g. of pork
116 g. of salsa criollo
500 ml. White broth
10 g of salt
Laurel (1 leaf)
3 g. of bija
30 ml. of oil
40 g. sweet red peppers (pimentos)
2 u. hard boiled eggs
4 g. minced parsley

## PREPARATION

Cut pork in about 4 cm pieces. Seal the meat in hot oil and cook a few minutes. Remove from fat and lightly fry the rice. Add the seasoning, the toasted and crushed herbs, the meat and broth and allow to boil. Add bija and salt and cook until completely done. Decorate with pimentos, hard boiled eggs and sprinkle cut parsley.

# Chicken and Rice

## INGREDIENTS

350 g. of rice
1 kg. of chicken
100 g. of onion
85 g. of peppers
100 g. fresh tomato
3 g. of bija
12 g. of garlic
60 ml. of dry White wine
1 laurel leaf
4 g. of cumin
4 g. of oregano
40 g. sweet red pepper (pimento)
2 u. egg
Peas
90 ml. of oil
600 ml. chicken stock
Salt to taste

## PREPARATION

Clean and cut the chicken in quarters. Season with salt and pepper. Peel and finely chop garlic, peppers and onion. Wasth the tomato and finely minced parsley. Heat the dry herbs and crush in a mortar with salt. Have the fat prepared. Stir fry the chicken without over cooking. Prepare chicken broth and add bija.

In hot oil add garlic, onion, pepper and tomato. Mix in a clay pot the lightly fried rice with the sauce and broth. Add the dry herbs and salt. Let cook until the grain begins to open; perfume with wine. Place the braised chicken on the rice. Decorate with pimentos, hard boiled eggs and peas.

# Rice with Cabbage

## INGREDIENTS

350 g. of rice
400 g. of cabbage
25 ml. of oil
30 g. of butter
500 ml. of water
Salt to taste

## PREPARATION

Pick and wash rice. Wash cabbage cut
a la jardiniere. Place water, oil, butter too
cook and when the cabbage is soft add to
the rice and stir. Let cook until finished.

# Rice with Corn

## INGREDIENTS

350 g. of rice
Tender corn
45 ml. of oil
90 g. of criolla sauce
3 g. of bija
60 ml. of dry white wine
500 ml. of water
Salt to taste

## PREPARATION

Shell corn. Prepare the criolla sauce.
Cook the corn until softened. Marinate
rice in hot oil. Add salsa criolla,
corn, bija and water. Dot with salt
and continue cooking until the rice is
completely softened. Finally perfume
with wine.

# Moros y Cristianos
## (Moors and Christians)

## INGREDIENTS

304 g. of rice
76 g. of black beans
460 ml. of water
24 g. of bacon (salt pork)
12 g. of salt
80 g. of onion
45 ml. of oil
60 g. of pimento
4 g. of oregano
1 laurel leaf
8 g. of garlic
4 g. of cumin
Salt to taste

## PREPARATION

Clean and wash beans. Soak in water for 10 to 12 hours approximately in the refrigerator. Soften at moderate heat in the same water used for soaking. Cut bacon, peel and cut onion and peppers in slices and the garlic finely chopped. In an appropriate bowl heat the oil and stir fry the bacon, garlic, onion and pepper. Add the oregano, cumin and laurel leaf. Add the softened beans with the broth used in cooking. Dot with salt. Clean and wash rice. Add when the water begins to boil. Stir and allow to boil until finished.

# Congrí Oriental

## INGREDIENTS

304 g. of rice
76 g. kidney beans
460 ml. of water
24 g. smoked pork
45 ml. of oil
232 g. of salsa criolla
1 laurel leaf
4 g. of oregano
4 g. cumin
Salt to taste

## PREPARATION

Pick, wash and soak the beans in water and place in refrigeration for 12 hours. Cook in the same water; stir fry the salt pork cut in slices in oil. Add herbs and sofrito criollo. Cook for 2 to 3 minutes. Add this seasoning to the beans when softened. Pick and wash rice and add to the beans; stir until boiling begins. Cover and let cook until finished.

# Rice with Black Eyed Beans

## INGREDIENTS

304 g. of rice
76 g. of black eyed beans
20 g. of bacon
35 g. of onion
6 g. of garlic
20 g. green pepper
45 ml. of oil
500 ml. of water
4 g. of oregano
Salt to taste

## PREPARATION

Cut bacon in small pieces. Cut onion and slice green pepper and garlic finely. Soak and soften the beans. Stir fry the bacon, garlic, onion and green pepper. Add the beans, rice and seasoning, salt and oregano Mix well. Cook until it begins to dry. Continue cooking until the rice is completely softened.

# Criollo Stew
## (Ajiaco a la criolla)

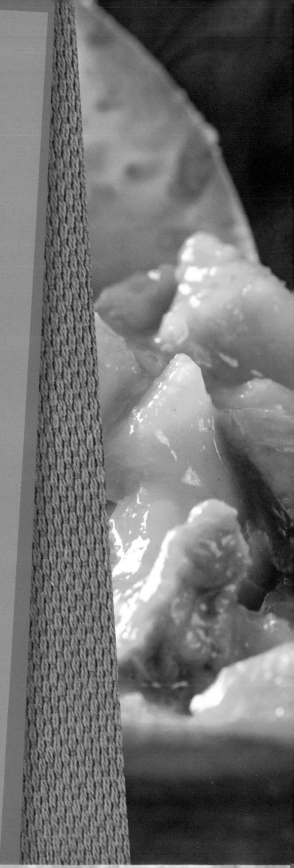

### INGREDIENTS

145 g. of beef jerky
145 g. Pig's head
87 g. of bacon
190 g. partially ripe plantain
190 g. of malanga
220 g. tender corn
220 g. of squash
220 g. of sweet potato
75 g. of criolla sauce
58 ml. of oil
2390 approximately of water
Salt to taste

### PREPARATION

Soak beef jerky for 12 hours approximately. Clean pig's head thoroughly and cut in pieces. Place beef jerky to cook in water for 30 minutes. Add pig head and let cook until softened. Later remove the meat and refresh. Bone head; clean beef jerky and cut in pieces of approximately 43 grams.

Strain the broth and add to the bullion previously used. Cook incorporating in order first the corn, let cook for 45 minutes' then the viands cut in pieces of 3 to 4 cm according to hardness, until softened.

Brown lightly the bacon and add to salsa criolla; to the stew and let cook for 10 more minutes.

# Vegetable Soup

## INGREDIENTS

188 g. of potatoes
145 g. of string beans
58 g. of celery
58 g. of leeks
58 g. cabbage
70 g. swiss chard
58 g. of onions
116 g. fresh tomato
3500 ml. vegetable broth
58 g. of butter
Salt to taste

## PREPARATION

Place in a bowl the butter. Add onions and soak. Add the cleaned vegetables cut in slices. In the case of the tomatoes, first pass over hot water to peel and continue with the same cuts. Stir continuously. Add the vegetable broth; let cook for 25 to 30 minutes approximately and season with salt. Serve in deep soup tureen.

# Rib meat Soup

## INGREDIENTS

240 g. of beef ribs
100 g. of potatoes
75 g. of noodles
8 g. of bell peppers
8 g. of onion
2 g. of garlic
8 g. of tomatoes
8 g. of tomato paste
4 g. of bija
1 laurel leaf
8 ml. of oil
3 liters of water
Salt to taste

## PREPARATION

Cut the ribs in portions. Cut onions, garlic cloves, bell peppers and tomatoes. Cut the potato in thin slices. Cook the ribs in water with salt. Stir fry the onions, peppers, garlic and tomatoes. Add seasoning, tomato paste diluted in water and laurel leaf. Let cook until the meat is tender. Remove ribs and separate the meat from the bones. Add potatoes and cook until softened. Add noodles and bija and continue cooking until the pasta is softened. Add the meat.

# Black Beans

## INGREDIENTS

551 g. of black beans
40 g. of bell peppers
6 g. of garlic
55 g. of onions
1 laurel leaf
4 g. of cumin
6 g. of sugar
55 ml. of oil
2 liters of water
Salt to taste

## PREPARATION

Pick and clean beans, wash and soak for 6 hours in refrigeration. Cook in the same water for 2 hours. Add laurel leaf, half of the bell pepper, garlic and onion cleaned and cut irregularly reserving the rest for later use. When the beans have softened add the other vegetables cut in slices and finely cut garlic, stir fried in oil the dry crushed roasted herbs.
Cook over low heat for approximately 25 minutes.

# Kidney Beans

### INGREDIENTS

220 g. of kidney beans
116 g. ham bone
220 g. of potatoes
42 g. of squash
24 g. of onions
40 g. of bacon
20 g. of chorizo
20 g. of tomatoes
12 g. of bell peppers
2 g. of garlic
45 ml. of oil
1280 ml. of water
4 g. of oregano
Salt to taste

### PREPARATION

Cut the bacon in fours after removing the skin and wash well.
Wash the ham bones. Skin the garlic and cut finely, skin onion and cut in fine strips. Remove the seeds of the bell peppers, cut in strips. Squeeze tomatoes and cut in this slices. Wash and cut the potatoes and cabbage in eighth parts potions. Heat the dry herbs and crush in a mortar. Pick clean the beans, Wash and soak for about 6 hours with the skin and bones in a pot. Begin cooking. Later add the potatoes and chorizo. Brown the bacon in the fat and add garlic, bell peppers, onions, tomatoes and dry herbs.
Remove the chorizo and cut in slices. Mix the chorizo and seasoning and add to the stew. Let cook for about 25 minutes. Serve in a deep dish.

# Roast Suckling Pig stuffed
## with moro rice

### INGREDIENTS

A piglet weighing from five to seven kilograms after cleaned and eviscerated is used for this dish
600 g. of seasoning to marinate
230 g. of oil
2 kg. approximately of Moors and Christian rice
800 g. fried pork portions
400 g. onion seasoning
Salt to taste

### PREPARATION

Make a small incision in the belly of the piglet and remove the intestines and other organs. Clean well. Remove the rib bones, backbone, hip and femur. Add salt and marinate with mojo seasoning. Let marinate approximately 12 hours.

Stuff with fried pork cut in regular portions. While roasting do not stuff full to leave space for the rice to grow.
Later sew the opening with a strong string, place on a baking sheet over wood planks to avoid sticking or on roasting pan.
Cross the legs and place face down. Brush with oil and repeat this operation often to brown.
Cover the ears and tail with aluminum foil and cook until the skin is toasted and crisp.
Serve with onion seasoning on top

# Fried Pork Chops

### INGREDIENTS

580 g. of pork chops
10 g. garlic
30 ml. of sour orange juice
116 g. onion seasoning
4 g. minced parsley
100 ml. of oil
Salt to taste

### PREPARATION

Place chops and lightly pound in a damp cloth. Season with salt, crushed garlic and sour orange juice.

Leave marinate in this seasoning for 3 to 4 hours. Heat oil in a frying pan and fry until browned on both sides. Serve with onion seasoning and minced parsley on top.

# Pork Head Stewed

### INGREDIENTS

852 g. head
1 laurel leaf
250 g. of salsa criolla
60 ml. oil

### PREPARATION

Select a pork head that is fresh. Clean and boil in water with laurel leaf and salt. When tender, remove and let refresh. Skin and cut meat in wide strips. Fry in hot fat for approximately 5 minutes. Add criolla sauce and let cook for 10 minutes until done.

# Crackling

## INGREDIENTS

1,400 g. crackling
120 ml. of water
Salt to taste

## PREPARATION

Cut pork skin in quarters and
slit fat parts. Cook the crackling.

# Gizzards

### INGREDIENTS

250 g. liver, kidneys, tongue and heart
10 g. of garlic
100 g. of onion
100 g. of bell pepper
40 ml. sour orange juice
300 g. tomato sauce
100 ml. oil
1 laurel leaf
60 ml. dry white wine
Salt and Pepper to taste

### PREPARATION

Clean and skin the gizzards chosen. Dice and marinate with the bell pepper, garlic, onion and sour orange juices for 2 to 4 hours.

Later season with pepper and salt to taste. Place in a pot with hot oil and let cook until browned. Stir fry onion, pepper or pimento and garlic. Add fresh herbs to the tomato sauce and sour orange juice. Cook for 5 minutes more and add browned gizzards and laurel leaf.

# Pork Fricassee

### INGREDIENTS

1044 g. meat interspersed with lard
116 g. tomato paste
60 g. fresh tomato
12 g. of garlic
4 g. paprika
1 laurel leaf
4 g. oregano
60 g. onion
40 ml. oil
60 ml. dry white wine
348 g. potatoes
36 g. bell peppers
2 g. sugar
Salt to taste

### PREPARATION

Cut meat in quarters, season with salt and pepper. Peel onions, the peppers, the potatoes and fresh tomatoes. Toast dry herbs and crush in mortar with the garlic.

Place the meat in a pot and cook. After browning, add onion, pepper, tomato, carrots, herbs, paprika and sugar. Let soak for 10 minutes and continue adding a liter of water. After boiling for a short time add potatoes and place in the oven until completely done. At the end finish with a splash of white wine. Let rest and remove fat before serving.

# Fricasseed Pork Feet

## INGREDIENTS

684 g. pork feet
348 g. of criolla sauce
60 ml. dry wine
Salt to taste

## PREPARATION

Cook the cleaned hoofs and remove the large bones. Cut in quarters of about 2 centimeters. Prepare sauce. In a pot mix the hooves with sauce and cook until done.

# Roast Pork Over Pit

## INGREDIENTS

1 80 pound pig
80 g. oregano
100 g. Cumin
60 g. Laurel leaf
200 g. garlic
3 liters of natural sour orange juice
Crushed white pepper
Salt to taste

## PREPARATION

Once slaughtered shave and clean. Open the belly towards the back hanks and remove the viscera. Marinate with salt, garlic sour orange, cumin and oregano. Let stand for 2 to 4 hours.

Insert pole the length of the animal. Sew the belly to prevent juices and seasoning from escaping

Open a pit of 2 meters long and approximately 50 cm deep. Introduce carbon in the pit and place a fork on both ends forming a "Y" that will hold the pole during the slow cooking which should last about 5 hours turning constantly.

On both ends place a closing on both ends and legs to prevent it from opening during the turns. Brush at intervals with the mojo

# Pork Sausages

## INGREDIENTS

464 g. leg of pork
232 g pork with fat streaks
116 g. of garlic
56 g. sweet paprika
4 g. of oregano
56 ml. of dry white wine
5 g. nutmeg
464 g. intestine strips
Salt to taste

## PREPARATION

Place the gut on the meat grinder with garlic. Have prepared the oregano, wine, salt and nutmeg. Keep macerated with the other ingredients for 48 hours. Fill the gut.

# Roast Steaks of pork

## INGREDIENTS

6440 g. pork leg meat
250 ml. of sour orange juice
30 g. of garlic
8 g. of oregano
15 g. cumin
2 laurel leaves
Salt to taste

## PREPARATION

Prepare seasoning with garlic, salt, oregano and sour orange juice. Marinate the pork for at least 12 hours. Place on a cooking tray and pour mojo over it. Cook for an hour and a half. After this time turn the leg, brush with mojo and continue cooking for another hour.

# Pork Stew

## INGREDIENTS

928 g. pork head and left overs of
roast pork
92 g. of onion
12 g. garlic
36 g. bell pepper
24 ml. dry wine
36 ml. of oil
Salt to taste

## PREPARATION

Cut head in pieces, remove large
bones and chop the skin and left overs
in the same manner. Peel the onion,
wash and cut in thick strips. Clean the
garlic cloves and mince. Wash the bell
peppers, remove the seeds and cut in
thick slices. Prepare ahead of time the
wine, salt and fat. Place in a roasting
pan over hot lard. Stir over the meat
the garlic, onion and peppers. When
all herbs are fried place the meat and
stir. Perfume with wine and dot with
salt.

# Fried Pork Pieces

## INGREDIENTS

624 g. clean thick steaks of pork
10 g. garlic
30 ml. juice of sour oranges
144 ml. vegetable oil
Salt to taste

## PREPARATION

Cut pork in 5 cm size pieces and season with
salt. Place over a thick bottomed pot with oil at
medium heat until browned. Peel and crush the
garlic, mix with sour orange juice and add 30
grams of hot oil, extract the meat from the fat.
Drain well and sprinkle with garlic seasoning.

# Criollo Style Minced Meat

## INGREDIENTS

464 g. beef
348 g. criollo seasoning
80 ml. of oil
60 g. of sweet red pepper
4 g. of minced parsley
Salt to taste

## PREPARATION

Clean meat and grind with medium size knife in a meat grinder. Season with salt. Stir fry in a frying pan with hot oil until separated. Reduce heat, add criollo seasoning and cook for about 5 minutes.

# Stewed Steak

### INGREDIENTS

1 kg. of meat
58 ml. oil
116 g. Criollo seasoning
58 ml. of dark bottom
4 g. minced parsley
Salt to taste

### PREPARATION

Cut meat in steak sizes of 250 gms each. Season with salt. In a partially deep pan place oil to heat. Fry the steaks until browned on both sides. Add wine, reduce and add the criollos seasoning. Cover and cook in moderate heat until done.

# Steak with Raw Seasonings

### INGREDIENTS

1 kg. beef rib cuts
58 ml. of oil
116 g. of onion
10 g. garlic
8 g. minced parsley
58 ml. of lemon juice
Salt to taste

### PREPARATION

Cut meat in 250 gm steaks. Lightly crush in a damp towel. Season with salt; macerate for a while with crushed garlic and lemon juice. Fry in a frying pan with oil or on a grill. Cook until it reaches the desired length of cooking. Cut onion and mince parsley and dot on top (raw mojo)

# Hot Ox Tail

### INGREDIENTS

1534 kg. ox tails
232 g. criollo seasoning
3 g. hot paprika
58 ml. of oil
43 g. smoked bacon
116 ml. dark bottom
20 ml. juice of sour oranges
10 g. crushed garlic
200 ml. red wine
90 ml. rum
Salt to taste

### PREPARATION

Cut tails at the joints. Wash, drain and marinate 2 to 4 hour with orange juices, salt and crushed garlic. Cut bacon in slices. Brown, add hot rum and wine. Reduce incorporating the rest of the marinade. Cover and let cook for 5 minutes after adding the paprika dusted over.
Add to dark bottom and stir fry criollos seasoning. Cover and place in the oven for two hours.

# Rags

## INGREDIENTS

464 g. of beef
10 g. garlic
116 g. onion
116 g. green bell peppers
116 ml. oil
1 laurel leaf
4 g. minced parsley
3 g. pepper slices
40 ml. dry wine
Salt to taste.

## PREPARATION

Cook meat in enough water with pepper grains, laurel leaf and salt. Strip the meat in filaments. Fry with half of the oil in hot skillet until slightly browned and add the peppers. With the rest of the oil stir fry the crushed garlic, onions and peppers cut in strips. Add meat; stir fry for a few minutes. Add the minced parsley.

# Tasajo (beef jerky)

## INGREDIENTS

600 g. tasajo
10 g. garlic
80 g. onions
150 ml. sour orange juice
60 ml. oil

## GARNISH

48 g. boiled sweet potato

## PREPARATION

Soak and boil tasajo two times changing the water. This process takes about two hours and a half. Peel, wash and cut onion in rings. Cut and juice sour oranges. Peel, wash and cook yucca. Chop the desalted tasajo in steak sizes. Crush to soften the texture and nerves that join the meat fibers. Marinate the tasajo with garlic, sour orange juice. Stir fry the onion and mix everything. Cook for about a minute.
Soak tasajo for two hours changing water frequently. Place tasajo in serving dish and add boiled sweet potato garnish.

# Fried cow

## INGREDIENTS

1160 g. cooked beef
20 g. garlic
192 g. onions
80 ml. sour orange juice
232 ml. oil
Salt to taste

## PREPARATION

Cut meat diagonally, form steaks of 145 g each. Slightly pound, prepare mojo with salt, crushed garlic and sour orange juice. Marinate in this mojo, Drain and fry at high heat on both sides. Stir fry in hot oil in a frying pat the onion cut in strips. Add extra mojo left over. Serve with the onions and mojo on top.

# Roast leg of Lamb

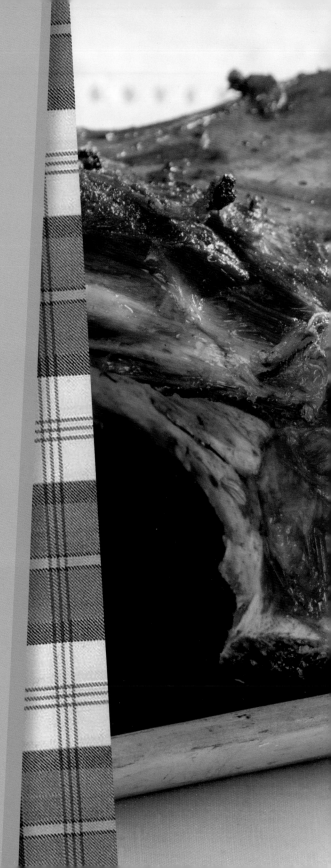

## INGREDIENTS

1 6 to 8 lbs leg of lamb
240 ml. oil
125 g. carrots
8 g. garlic
200 g. onion
200 g. fresh tomatoes
20 g. celery
1 laurel leaf
4g. oregano
90 ml. dry wine
Salt to taste

## PREPARATION

Bone the leg of lamb. Marinate with crushed garlic, salt, laurel leaf, oregano, sliced carrots, celery, onion cut in rings and wine for 3 hours minimum. Cook until the meat is tender. Once cooked, place in a serving dish to refresh to room temperature. Extract juice from the cooking procedure and strain. Once cold the roast leg of lamb is cut in slices, heated with the addition of sauce or juice.

# Lamb in Peppers and Tomatoes

## INGREDIENTS

1288 g. of lamb
40 g. onion
40 g. bell peppers
8 g. garlic
46 g. fresh tomatoes
38 g. tomato paste
58 ml. oil
1 laurel leaf
4 g. oregano
6 g. red pimentoes
2 g. garlic
100 ml. White broth
Salt to taste

## PREPARATION

Cut the lamb in regular pieces, Marinate in mojo made with wine, crushed garlic, salt, oregano and laurel leaf.
Brown lamb in hot oil, add crushed garlic, onion, bell peppers cut in strips, fresh tomatoes cut the same way, tomato paste, broth and the rest of the mojo. Cover and place it over at moderate heat for 1 hour. Served decorated with slices of pimentoes and peas.

# Roast Rabbit

## INGREDIENTS

1500 g. of rabbit
50 ml. vegetable oil
650 ml. of marinade for the
rabbit

## PREPARATION

Place the marinade in a deep
pot and place the rabbit on top.
Roast in a rustic oven for 1 hour
(brush the rabbit often with the
liquid of the marinade) and
strain the juice over it to remove
fat.

### Note

MARINADE: crushed garlic,
leeks and scallions, sour orange
juice, vegetable oil, celery, laurel
leaf, salt and pepper.

# Rabbit a la Campesina

## INGREDIENTS

1140 g. rabbit
72 g. oil
4 g. garlic
120 ml. homemade wine
184 g. onion
44 g. bell peppers
44 g. tomato paste
184 g. of bacon
Salt to taste

## PREPARATION

Clean and quarter the rabbit. Add salt. Pepare garlic, onion, peppers cut in fine slices. Place the pieces of rabbit to marinate and add wine. In a fryer or pot, fry the rabbit lightly. In another heat fat add the ingredients of the marinade and rabbit meat. Cover with broth and cook until tender.

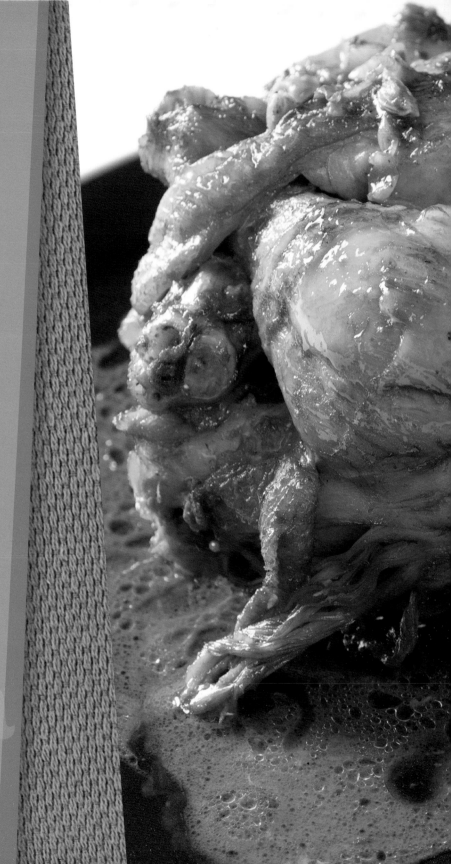

# Roast Chicken

## INGREDIENTS

720 g. of chicken
20 ml. sour orange juice
20 ml. oil
4 g. garlic
4 g. oregano
4 g. cumin
60 g. onion
90 ml. dry white wine
Salt to taste

## PREPARATION

Cut the chicken in eighths and marinade with salt, oregano, garlic and sour orange juice. Cut onions in slices and place in an oiled pot. On top place the chicken pieces. Cook over low heat and frequently brush with the resulting sauce. Continue cooking until tender.

# Minced Gizzards

## INGREDIENTS

336 g. gizzards
48 ml. of criolla sauce
30 ml. oil
52 ml. dry white wine
Salt to taste

## PREPARATION

Wash and clean the gizzards, grind and season with salt. Prepare the criolla sauce. Lightly stir fry the ground gizzards. Add the criolla sauce. Add wine at the end.

# Country Style Chicken

## INGREDIENTS

500 g. of chicken
100 ml. of criolla sauce
20 ml. dry white wine
20 ml. oil
Salt to taste

## PREPARATION

Cut and season the chicken with salt. Cook in water until tender. Remove the pieces and bone. Prepare the criolla sauce. Stir fry the pieces of chicken, adding the criolla sauce. At the end add the wine.

# Stewed Hen

## INGREDIENTS

528 g. of hen
30 ml. of oil
150 g. potatoes
40 ml. criolla sauce
32 ml. dry white wine
340 ml. poultry broth
4 g. paprika
4 g. ground white pepper
Salt to taste

## PREPARATION

Remove excess fat and cut hen in quarters and eighths according to size. Prepare the criolla sauce and poultry broth. Stir fry hen pieces, adding the broth with salt cooking until completely tender. Add the potatoes cut in quarters, criolla sauce, and paprika and continue cooking until potatoes are done. Add the wine at the end.

# Fried Chicken

## INGREDIENTS

4 chicken halves partially boned
116 g. mojo for marinade
116 g. onion mojo
4 g. minced parsley
230 ml. oil
Salt to taste

## PREPARATION

Cut chicken from the loin in two boned halves. Season with salt and marinate for 2 to 3 hours win mojo marinade. Fry in hot oil on both sides (first place the side with skin down and then turn when browned.
Serve with onion mojo on top, powder with minced parsley.

# Turkey Fricassee

### INGREDIENTS

480 g. turkey
200 g. potatoes
60 ml. criolla sauce
100 ml .oil
100 ml. dry white wine
332 ml. poultry broth
Salt to taste

### PREPARATION

Cut turkey in serving sizes. Cut the potatoes in quarters. Prepare the poultry broth and criolla sauce. Stir fry turkey pieces adding the broth and cooking until completely tender. Add the potatoes, salt, criollo sauce and continue cooking until the potatoes are done. Add wine at the end.

# Stuffed Turkey

### INGREDIENTS

556 g. turkey
1 kg moro rice
30 ml. oil
15 g. onion
4 g. ground White pepper
60 ml. lemon
10 g. garlic
Salt to taste

### PREPARATION

Bone the turky. Season with salt, pepper, onion, garlic and lemon. Fill with Moro rice and sew closed. Brush with oil and place in the oven or large pot at low heat. Brush with juice until completed
.

### Note

For the preparation of Moro rice find in the recipes for rices.

# Fricasseed Eggs

## INGREDIENTS

4 eggs
80 g. criolla sauce
Salt to taste

## PREPARATION

Select eggs. Prepare criolla sauce. Heat water to boiling point. Place eggs. Let cool and peel and cut in half. Add criolla sauce.

Note: For scrambled eggs it is prepared the same way as well as in an omelet. The eggs are beaten and cooked with low oil. The scrambled egg can be added to kinds of meats, sausages or cheese.

# Fried Egg

### INGREDIENTS

4 eggs
45 ml. oil
Salt to taste

### PREPARATION

Crack eggs. Heal oil and add.
Remove and drain well. Sprinkle
with salt.

# Natural Omelet

### INGREDIENTS

270 g. eggs
20 ml. oil
Salt to taste

### PREPARATION

Beat eggs and add salt. Heat oil
and add beaten eggs. Turn the omelet
when almost completely cooked taking
care not to burn it.

Omelet's can also be made with
potatoes, plantains or used with
sausages.

# Campesino Salad

## INGREDIENTS

116 g. potatoes
116 g. carrots
116 g. bell peppers
8 eggs
20 g. cooking tomato
Salt to taste
120 g. mayonnaise

## PREPARATION

Wash and cut potatoes,
carrots, pimentos and tomatoes
in strips. Boil the eggs and
refresh to peel. Cut two eggs
in half slices. The other half
sliced. Prepare mayonnaise.
Mix all in a deep dish with
the mayonnaise Decorate
artistically.

# Green Bean Salad

### INGREDIENTS

600 g. green beans
Salad dressing

### PREPARATION

Wash and cut beans; Cook in low
amount of water. Drain and place on a
salad dish. Add dressing.

# Corn Fritters

## INGREDIENTS

425 g. tender corn
2 eggs
40 ml. oil
Salt to taste

## PREPARATION

Grind corn. Mix well with salt
and the eggs. Take a spoonful
and drop on hot oil. Cook until
the fritters are nicely browned.

# Corn Stew with Pork

### INGREDIENTS

580 g. of pork
232 g. tender rice kernels
232 g. potatoes
232 g. criolla sauce
500 ml. of broth
30 ml. oil
6 g. garlic
4 g. cumin
Salt to taste

### PREPARATION

Cut pork in 4 cm pieces. Season with salt, pepper and crushed garlic. Seal the meat in hot oil Add corn, let cook several minutes and add potatoes.

# Tamal in Leaves

## (in other parts of the island they are called hallacas or hayacas)

### INGREDIENTS

500 g. tender or ground corn
500 g. pork
116 ml. Oil
232 g. criolla sauce
Salt to taste

### PREPARATION

Cut pork in 2 cm pieces. Have criolla sauce prepared. Stir fry the pork in oil to brown. Add the sauce and mix with the corn. Dot with salt.
Using the corn leaves make a cone to hold the corn. Cover with another leaf folding the tamal. Tie in corn strips or string knotting in the center.
Place a pot with water and salt. Cook the tamales for about 30 minutes. Remove from water and serve having removed half of the leaves. They can be served with hot sauce or ketchup.

Note: The tamales can be tied with strips from the corn leaves or with string. In Cuba it is done in different manners and has different names. In the eastern region they are known as Ayacas.

# Corn Meal

### INGREDIENTS

620 g. corn flour
260g. criolla sauce
45 ml. oil
2, 5 liters of water
Salt to taste

### PREPARATION

PPrepare a criolla sauce. Boil water with salt. Add corn meal and let cook until it thickens. Add the criolla sauce and oil. Continue cooking until an adequate consistency is achieved.

# Stewed Tamal with Pork

### INGREDIENTS

500 g. tender corn meal
500 g. pork
116 ml. oil
232 g. criolla sauce
250 ml. White broth or water
Salt to taste

### PREPARATION

Mix the corn meal with broth or water at room temperature. Strain. Cut the pork in 4 cm pieces. Season with salt. Fry gently in hot oil until well done. Add the meat to the corn meal as well as the criolla sauces. Mix well. Dot with salt. Cook at slow heat until thickened stirring with a wooden spoon.

# Fried Ripe Plantain

## INGREDIENTS

920 g. plantain
90 ml. oil

## PREPARATION

Peel the plantain and cut ends.
Cut in transversal slices of about 1
cm thickness. Add to hot oil and
turn to prevent burning. Remove
and drain.

# Fried Sweet Potato

## INGREDIENTS

860 g. sweet potato
90 ml. oil
Salt to taste

## PREPARATION

Wash sweet potato well with a brush Peel, cut in slices of 8 cm. Soak in water. Add to hot oil in slow heat until golden brown. Remove and drain.

# Roasted Sweet Potato

## INGREDIENTS

400 g. sweet potato
36 ml. lard
60 g. butter
Salt to taste

## PREPARATION

Seleccionar los boniatos medianos y sanos. LavaSelect medium size sweet potatoes. Wash well with a brush and cut in 2cm thick slices. Set water to boil in a pot with a dash of salt. When it begins to boil add the slices of sweet potato.
Cover the pot and cook at medium heat until tender without crumbling. Remove the water and let cook until golden brown on both sides. Add pieces of butter cover and continue cooking at low heat until golden brown.

Note: if desired 45 g of sugar can be added to glaze the sweet potatoes. It is quite delicious.

# Chatino Plantains

## INGREDIENTS

480 g. plantains
176 ml. oil
Salt to taste

## PREPARATION

Peel the plantains eliminating the ends. Cut in rounds of 3 to 4 cm thickness. Add to hot oil for approximately 7 minutes. Remove, drain and crush until leaving them 1 cm thick. Raise the temperature of the oil and add the crushed plantains for about 80 seconds.

# Mashed plantains

## INGREDIENTS

400 g. of plantains
120 g. Pork pieces
3 lt. of water
200 ml. fowl broth
4 g. garlic
Salt to taste

## PREPARATION

Peel the plantains, cut in 3 parts and place in water with lemon. Cut the pork in squares of 2 cm and fry until it resembles crackling. Peel the garlic and cut finely or crush. Grind the plantains or crush with a fork. Add the garlic to the pork. Add broth and let cook 10 minutes at 95o C.. Mix with pork pieces, garlic and broth.

# Plantain Chipa

## INGREDIENTS

292 g. of plantains
60ml. of oil
Salt to taste

## PREPARATION

Peel plantains and slice thinly either manually or electrically. Introduce in hot oil (110o C) for about 8 minutes. Use a slotted spoon to prevent them from sticking during the cooking. Remove and drain. Season.

# Malanga Fritters

## INGREDIENTS

240 g. of malanga
6 ml. oil to mix
460 ml. de oil to fry
6 g. garlic
1 egg
Salt to taste

## PREPARATION

Peel and grate raw malanga.
Crush garlic and beat egg. Mix
all ingredients including the 6 ml
of oil. Gather a spoonful of this
mixture and add to hot oil. Fry
until golden brown.

# Malanga Puree

### INGREDIENTS

535 g. of malanga
80 ml. of milk
20 g. of butter
Salt to taste

### PREPARATION

Peel and cut malanga into pieces, cook in water with salt. When soft remove from water and reduce to the consistency of puree. Add milk and butter. Mix all until the required consistency is achieved.

# Boiled Ñame

### INGREDIENTS

11000 g. of ñame
140 g. seasoning for viands
Salt to taste

### PREPARATION

Cut ñame in pieces. Prepare seasoning for viands. Cook ñame in water with salt until softened. Remove from water and add seasoning.

# Yucca with mojo
## (seasoning)

### INGREDIENTS

400 g. of yucca
70 g. seasoning for viands
(mojo)
Salt to taste

### PREPARATION

Cut yucca into pieces.
Prepare the mojo. Cook yucca
in water with salt. And when
soft remove from water and
add mojo.

# Fried Yucca

## INGREDIENTS

1800 g. of yucca
70 ml. of oil
Salt to taste

## PREPARATION

Cut yucca in pieces. And cook in
water with salt until soft. Drain well.
Fry yucca pieces until golden brown.

# Squash Puree

## INGREDIENTS

560 g. of squash
15 ml. oil
2 g. garlic
Salt to taste

## PREPARATION

Cut squash in square pieces of about
6 cm. Finely chop garlic. Cook squash
in water with salt. Stir-fry the garlic
lightly in oil. Make a puree and garlic
and oil on top.

# Mango Juice

## INGREDIENTS

8 ripe mangoes
1 litre of water
Sugar to taste

## PREPARATION

Peel mangos and cut pulp and blend with a Little water. Drain and add water and sugar.

### Note

The method used to process the mango can be used for other fruits such as pineapple, guava and papaya.

# Garapiña

## INGREDIENTS

280 g. pineapple rind
112 g. sugar
1 lt. of water

## PREPARATION

Place rinds in a glass or clay jar with 2 tablespoons of sugar, without mixing. Cover with cheesecloth to allow air to penetrate. Ferment for 2 days. Add remaining sugar and mix. Drain and serve cold.

# Beverage of Cañandonga

## INGREDIENTS

100 g. of cañandonga
1 lt. of water
50 g. sugar

## PREPARATION

Cut cañandonga and extract pulp with seeds. Place in blender adding water. Drain and add sugar. Serve cold

Note: The cañandonga or cañafístula cimarrona is a plant abundant in Camagüey and Guantánamo. It is a large copious tree with green leaves. The fruit is a cylindrical pod about a yard long and is filled with flat packed seeds. It has a dark substance that is sweet and is the edible part

# Champola

## INGREDIENTS

520 g. pulp of guanábana
500 ml. of milk
Add sugar as desired

## PREPARATION

Mix guanábana pulp with milk. Sweeten and serve cold

# Granada Beverage

## INGREDIENTS

250 g. ripe granada
150 g. of sugar
1 lt. of water

## PREPARATION

Cut granada and extract pulp and seeds, add sugar and mix adding water. Drain. Serve cold.

# Rice Pudding

## INGREDIENTS

60 g. of rice
350 ml. of water
160 ml. of milk
90 g. of sugar
1 cinnamon stick
3 g. de lemon rind
5 g. of vanilla
20 g. powdered cinnamon
Salt as wished

## PREPARATION

Clean and wash rice. Prepare beforehand sugar, fresh milk, cinnamon, salt and vanilla, green lemon rind and water. Place rice in a pot with water until softened. In another bowl place milk, cinnamon stick and sugar. Cook and let boil for 3 minutes. Place and incorporate the rice. Add the lemon rind and allow to boil stirring constantly for 30 minutes. Add vanilla and remove from heat. Let refresh. Present in a dessert dish adding powdered cinnamon. Keep in fresh place.

# Yucca Fritters

### INGREDIENTS

464 g. of yucca
232 g. of malanga (can be substituted with sweet potato)
Sal to taste
25 g. eggs
Cinnamon as desired
Anise as desired
Lemon rind as desired
35 g. flour
Oil for frying
232 ml. syrup

### PREPARATION

Cook until softened the yucca and malanga. Let cool, drain and grind to make a puree. Add salt, and a mix made with cinnamon, anise, lemon rind, beaten egg. Knead over a table brushed with flour and form little rods of about 87 grams each. Form an 8 figure. Let rest a few minutes. Fry in hot oil until golden brown. Let freshen and served with syrup.

# Papaya Pieces in Syrup

### INGREDIENTS

400 g. of papaya
280 g. of sugar
2 l. of water
Salt to taste

### PREPARATION

Wash fruit and cut in medium size pieces. Cook until softened. Remove from heat and add sugar. Cook at moderate heat until the syrup acquires the desired density.

# Boniatillo

### INGREDIENTS

500 g. sweet potato
500 g. sugar
44 g. yolk of egg
10 g. lemon
10 g. butter
10 ml. dry white wine
300 ml. water
Salt as desired

### PREPARATION

CCut pieces of sweet potatoes. Cook in water until softened. Make syrup with water, sugar and lemon juice. Mash to puree consistency adding syrup little by little and mix well. Add the beaten egg yolk and salt. Cook mixing constantly until thickened. Add butter and wine at the end.

# Guava Halves in Syrup

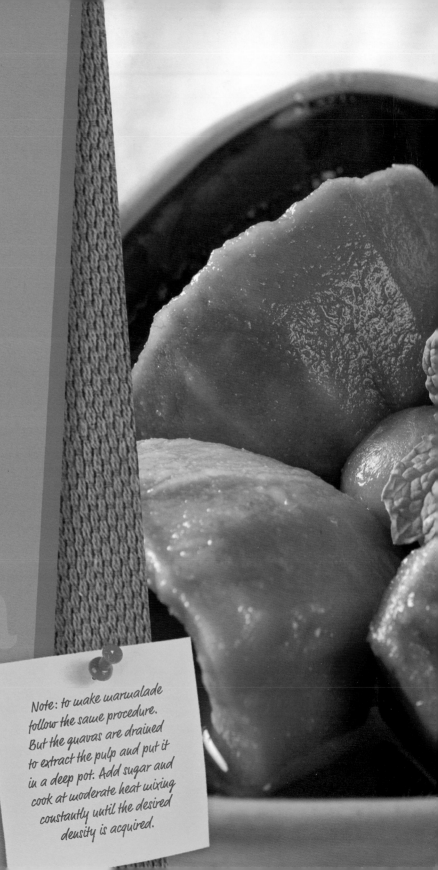

## INGREDIENTS

1450 kg. guava halves
928 ml. water
1305 g. of sugar
Salt as desired

## PREPARATION

Select semi ripe guavas with thick skin. Peel, cut in half and remove seeds. IN a proper pot add the guava halves with enough water and boil until softened. Use 928 ml. of the cooking water. Add sugar and salt and boil for 20 more minutes. Serve cold.

Note: to make marmalade follow the same procedure. But the guavas are drained to extract the pulp and put it in a deep pot. Add sugar and cook at moderate heat mixing constantly until the desired density is acquired.

# Orange Halves

## INGREDIENTS

400 g. of oranges
240 g. sugar
144 ml. water for the syrup

## PREPARATION

Wash and peel oranges. Cut in quarters and remove pulp with seeds ending up with thin quarters like a canoe. Dip in water and put to boil. Remove the water of the first boil. And continue boiling as much as wanted to remove the bitter taste and are soft. Prepare light syrup in a deep pot. Add the orange halves until the proper density es achieved.

# Cusubé

## INGREDIENTS

384 g. yucca starch
92 g. sugar
1 egg
36 g. pork lard
3 g. anisette toasted and crushed
1 g. powdered cinnamon
36 ml. white wine

## PREPARATION

Mix all the ingredients in a bowl to obtain a compact mass. Take small portions and make rectangular shapes. With the knife handle mark the surface with two crosses and place in a buttered pan. Cook until golden brown for 30 minutes.

# Squash Flan

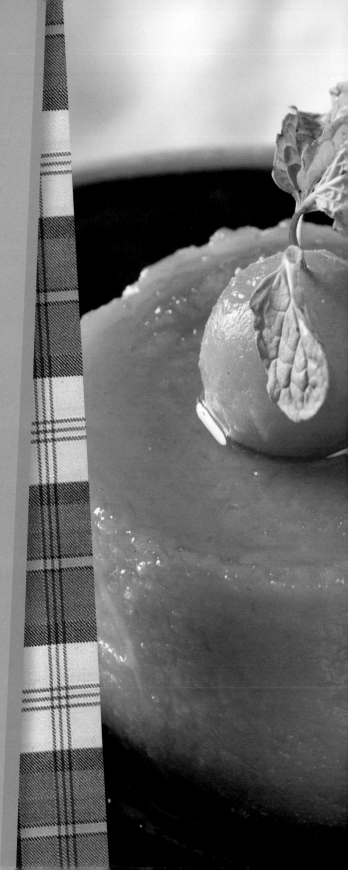

### INGREDIENTS

172 g. squash
128 ml. milk
80 g. sugar
88 g. of eggs
12 g. cornstarch
4 g. vanilla
Dash of salt

### PARA EL CARAMELO

20 g. of sugar
8 ml. of water

### PREPARATION

Cut squash in pieces. Dissolve cornstarch in
a small amount of milk. Prepare the caramel
adding a small amount of water before softening.
Prepare the milk. Cook the squash in a little
amount of water until softened. Eliminated the
rind and reduce to a puree. Add milk, dissolved
cornstarch, the beaten eggs, the sugar and salt.
Mix well and strain. Add vanilla and pour into
a mold previously bathed with the caramel.
Place the mold in a double boiler and cook
preventing it to boil.

# Majarete

### INGREDIENTS

372 g. tender ground corn
½ liter fresh milk
192 g. sugar
1 cinnamon stick
Grated lemon rind
Dash of salt

### PREPARATION

Mix corn with milk, strain and add remaining ingredients. Cook revolving constantly until thickened. Remove for the fire and pour in dessert dish. Powder with cinnamon.

# Malarrabia

### INGREDIENTS

400 g. of sweet potato
1 l. molasses
3 g. cinnamon sticks
3 u. tender orange leaves

### PREPARATION

Peel and wash sweet potato. Cut in strips (2 x 2cm) and cook in 1 liter of water until it begins to soften. Cover with molasses adding the cinnamon and orange leaves. Continue cooking until the sweet potato is softened and the syrup concluded.

# Corn Meal with Coconut

### INGREDIENTS

92 g. dry cornmeal
1 l. of water
1 u. cinnamon stick
1 g. aniseed
120 g. sugar
200 ml. of milk
28 g. butter a
80 g. shredded coconut
Dash of salt

### PREPARATION

Mix shredded coconut with sugar and half a liter of water. Cook letting it boil until thickened. Stir constantly. Wash and strain the cornmeal and cook with half a liter of water, salt, cinnamon, aniseed until soft and thick. Add the cocoanut preparation to the cornmeal and cook over moderate heat stirring frequently until the thickness desired is obtained. Remove from fire and refresh. Serve cold.

# Brown Coconut

## INGREDIENTS

3 dry coconuts
240 g. of Brown sugar
120 ml. Honey
60 ml. of water

## PREPARATION

Grind coconut and place in pot with the sugar, water and Honey. Cook in slow heat stirring constantly. Stop cooking when it acquires a thick consistency. Let refresh for a few minutes and pour over wax paper with a spoon.

Note: For white coconut the same procedure is followed only White sugar is used.

# Coconut and Mint Pudding

## INGREDIENTS

400 g. pulp of dry coconut
3 u. eggs
140 g. of sugar
24 g. butter
384 g. shredded fresh bread
80 g. toasted peanuts
3 g. de lemon rind
Dash of salt
1 l. of water

## PREPARATION

Grate coconut adding one liter of water, Let rest 10 minutes. Add to cheesecloth and press removing the milk. Wet the shredded bread to this milk to soften. Add the shredded coconut with the bread shreds. Add beaten eggs, melted butter, sugar, toasted peanuts and lemon grated lemon rind.

Mix all the ingredients until a homogenous mass is obtained. Pour over a buttered pan and bake for 45 minutes approximately. Remove from oven and let refresh. Unmold and keep in refrigeration. Served bathed in syrup or covered with scorched merengues.

# Coconut Desert in Syrup

## INGREDIENTS

460 g shredded coconut
400 g sugar
250 ml. water
5 g cinnamon stick

## PREPARATION

Cook coconut in water with cinnamon for 15 minutes at moderate heat until soft. Add sugar and mix constantly until the syrup is thickened.

# Criollo Coffee

### INGREDIENTS

60 g. Coffee poder
300 ml. water

### PREPARATION

Place pot with water to heat.
When hot add the Coffee and
Stir. When boiling begins pore
in the cloth sleeve. Add sugar
according to taste.

# Carretero Coffee

Is the rustic manner of preparation, typical of rural zones. After boiling, the coffee is not strained but only let the grounds settle. Often used a piece of hot carbon is placed that aids in decanting it. It is also called a very strong coffee if not strained and without sugar. A fast way to prepare.

## SLEEVE:

Traditional Manner of making criollo Coffee through a sleeve. Also called Tetera. It is used to strain mixtures of boiling water with coffee. Specially made with cloth that is placed under an aluminum, stainless steel or enamel jar.

# Aguachirri

Name of watered Coffee and also all drinks with undefined tastes. In some regions the grounds are again strained and sweetened. This traditional drink is given to children.

# Complementary Recipes

### ADOBO CRIOLLO (criollo seasoning)

*INGREDIENTS*

2 g. laurel leaves
2 g. oregano
20 g. garlic
250 g. juice of sour oranges
15 g. salt

*PREPARATION*

Crush garlic in a mortar with the herbs and salt. At the end add the juice of the sour orange.

### COMMON SEASONING

*INGREDIENTS*

180 g. OIL
230 g. juice of lemon or sour oranges
30 g. of salt

*PREPARATION*

Mix all ingredients. Save covered in refrigeration and stir before use.

### SEASONING FOR SALADS

*INGREDIENTS*

375 g. OIL
125 g. Vinegar
7 g. salt

*PREPARATION*

Mix all ingredients and keep in refrigeration covered. Stir before using.

### RAW SEASONING

*INGREDIENTS*

180g. Oil
115g. juice of lemon or sour orange
15 g. garlic
90 g. water
15 g. salt

*PREPARATION*

Dissolve salt in juice. Add minced garlic and oil. Mix well. Keep covered in refrigeration and stir before use.

### RAW MOJO

*INGREDIENTS*

180 g. oil
60 g. juice of lemon or sour orange
85 g. bell pepper
20 g. garlic
100 g. onion
14 g. salt

*PREPARATION*

Dissolve salt in juice. Add bell pepper, garlic and onion finely chopped. Add oil and mix well. Keep In refrigeration and stir before using.

### TOMATO MOJO

*INGREDIENTS*

210 g. skinned ripe tomatoes without seeds and chopped in rather thick pieces
45 g. juice of lemon or sour oranges
8 g. finely minced garlic
60 g. finely minced onions
5 g. salt

*PREPARATION*

Add lemon, onion, garlic and salt to the ripe tomato, especially good for fried or boiled eggs, grilled or fried fish, tamal In leaves etc.

# MAYONAISE

### INGREDIENTS

500 ml. vegetable oil
3 ó 4 egg yolks (approximately 60 grams))
6 g. salt
20 ml. vinegar or lemon juice
10 g. mustard
0, 5 g. crushed white pepper

### PREPARATION

In a blender jar add egg yolks, mustard, pepper, salt and half of the vinegar or lemon juice. Beat adding oil little by little while beating. When thickened you can add oil more rapidly. Lastly add the rest of the vinegar, reduced and hot or lemon juice at room temperature.

---

# MOJOS FOR VIANDS

### INGREDIENTS

87 g. oil
450 g. Juice of sour oranges
50 g. garlic
200 g. water
20 g. salt

### PREPARATION

Crush garlic in a mortar. Add salt and crush until a paste is formed. Dilute in water and sour orange juice. Heat in hot oil at 190ºC, Rapidly add the crushed garlic and cover immediately.

# SWEET AND SOUR SAUCE

### INGREDIENTS

58 g. pickled cucumbers
90 g. green bell peppers
90 g. red bell peppers
87 g. pineapple
58 g. onion
58 g. oil
5 g. ginger
143 ml. vinegar
116 g. red currant jelly or sugar
145 g. tomato paste
100 ml. chicken or fish broth
15 g. cornstarch
87 g. carrots
58 g. peas
4 g. salt

### PREPARATION

Cut finely in julienne slices the onion, peppers, cucumber, pineapple, carrots and ginger, Stir fry in hot oil adding the ingredients in this order. Add vinegar and reduce adding the red currant jam or sugar, tomato paste to the 1/3of the reserved broth to dilute cornstarch. Add, boil 2 minutes stirring constantly. Dot with salt and add the peas.

---

# CRIOLLO SEASONING

### INGREDIENTS

10 g. garlic
116 g. onions
87 g. bell peppers
220 g. fresh tomatoes
100 g. tomato paste
1 laurel leaf
1 g. ground pepper
20 g. salt
58 ml. dry white wine
35 ml. vegetable oil

### PREPARATION

Cut and peel the garlic. Peel and clean onions, peppers cut in thin slices. Remove seeds from the tomatoes and cut the same although a little thicker. In a deep pot heat the oil. When hot stir fry the garlic, onion, pepper, tomatoes, tomato paste, laurel leaf, pepper and salt. Boil 10 minutes.
In a separate pot reduce wine and add to the sauce.

---

# Technical Vocabulary

**Adobo:** Marinade prepared with salt, oil, garlic, sour oranges or vinegar and herbs.

**Ahumar:** Smoke. Expose food to smoke to dry and give it a characteristic taste or to prepare for conservation.

**Aliñar:** Season a preparation .

**Blanquear:** Soften. Place greens or meats in boiling water for a few minutes without cooking.

**Escaldar:** Place in boiling water for a few minutes. .

**Fondo:** Extract obtained from cooking mollusks, and crustaceans, fish, meat or greens. Serves as a base for sauces and soups.

**Fondo oscuro:** Rib bones browned in the oven and mixed with seasoning browned in fat and boiled together in water for a long period of time.

**Juliana (a la):** Applied to define any product cut in fine strips (about 3 to 5 cm long by 1 to 3 thick)

**Lonja:** Long, wide and thick piece

**Macerar:** Place food into a liquid mixture of aromatic herbs and adobos, wine, liquiers, sugar as required

**Marinada:** Marinade in liquid with herbs and spices (wine, lemon juice, vinegar, sour milk and butter Used to conserve and soften meat and fish. Also usted in some sauces for salads.

**Pochar:** Poach

**Reducir:** Boil a sauce, broth, etc. to make tastier by evaporating excess liquid Boil to the consistency of syrup

**Roux:** It is the base for any sauce. It is a mixture of flour and butter in a proportion of 50 g of butter to 50 g of flour lightly cooked in moderate heat and stirring constantly with a wooden pallet or spoon

**Basic white sauce or Bechamel:** Basic sauce of butter, four, nutmeg, salt and pepper. Used to accompany eggs, potatoes, asparagus, cauliflower, broccoli, fish, shell fish, pastas, chicken, etc.

**Salsa criolla:** Common sauce prepared with oil (or lard), garlic, onion, bell peppers, parsley, tomato, salt and pepper and broth desired.

**Saltear:** Stir fry in oil at high heat mixing constantly.

**Sellar:** Seal or lightly brown meat pieces in boiling oil to prevent losing juices during the rest of the cooking procedure.

**Trinchar:** Cut pieces to be served in the table.

# Equivalent Weights and Measures

1 ounce = 28,75 g
1 liquid ounce = 30 cc = 30 g
1 cup = 8 ounces = 240 g = 16 tablespoons
1 pint = 2 cups = 16 ounces
1 tablespoon = 15 g = 3 teaspoons
1 teaspoon = 5 g = 60 drops
1 pound = 460 g = 16 ounces
1 liter = 4 cups = 32 ounces = 960 g
½ liter = 1 pint = 2 cups = 16 ounces
1 bottle = 3 cups = 24 = ounces = 0,725 liters
1 Kg = 1000 g = 2,2 pounds
1 toneladas = 20 quintales = 2 000 libras

1 quintal = 4 arrobas
1 arroba = 25 libras
1 galón = 4 litros
1 gramo = 1000 microgramos
1 pound white sugar = 2½ cups
1 pound raw rice = 2 cups
1 pound cooked rice = approximately 7 cups
1 pound of raw beans = 2 cups
1 can of condensed milk = 15 ounces= 400 g = $1^{1/3}$ cups
1 can of evaporated milk = $1^{2/3}$ cups = 411g = 13 ounces
1 pound of powdered milk = 4 liters
1 pound of flour = 4 cups

# Table of equivalents

| PRODUCT | MEASURES | WEIGHT |
|---|---|---|
| Oil | One splash | 5 ml |
| | 1 teaspoon | 8 ml |
| | 1 tablespoon | 18 ml |
| Rice | 1 small cup | 125 gms |
| | 1 cup | 250 gms |
| Common Sugar | 1 dash | 1 gm |
| | 1 teaspoon | 5 gms |
| | 1 tablespoon | 15 gms |
| | 1 cup | 250 gms |
| Powdered sugar (glace) | 1 teaspoon | 2 gms |
| | 1 tablespoon | 6 gms |
| | 1 cup | 100 gms |
| Liquids | 1 teaspoon | 5 ml |
| | 1 tablespoon | 15 ml |
| | 1 cup | 250 ml |
| Butter (fat) | 1 teaspoon | 5 gms |
| | 1 tablespoon | 15 gms |